How to
Housebreak
and
Train
Your Dog
by Arthur Liebers

Published by T.F.H. Publications, Inc., TFH Building, 245 Cornelison Avenue, Jersey City, N. J. 07302. Distributed in the British Empire by T.F.H. Publications (London), Ltd., 13 Nutley Lane, Reigate, Surrey, England. In Canada, to the Pet Trade by Canadian Aquarium Supply Co. and Viobin of 1125 Talbot Street, St. Thomas, Ontario, Canada. In Canada, to the Book Trade, by Clarke, Irwin & Company Limited, Clarwin House, 791 St. Clair Avenue West, Toronto 10, Ontario, Canada. Printed in the U.S.A. by the lithograph process by T.F.H. Lithograph Corp., Jersey City, N. J. 07302.
Distributed to the Book Trade in the U.S.A. by Sterling Publishing Co., New York, N. Y. 10016.

TITLES IN THIS SERIES
(some still in preparation)

How to Raise and Train a COCKER SPANIEL
How to Raise and Train a POODLE
How to Raise and Train a GERMAN SHEPHERD
How to Raise and Train a BOXER
How to Raise and Train a COLLIE
How to Raise and Train an AFGHAN
How to Raise and Train a CHIHUAHUA
How to Raise and Train a DACHSHUND
How to Raise and Train a BEAGLE
How to Raise and Train a MINIATURE SCHNAUZER
How to Raise and Train a DOBERMAN PINSCHER
How to Raise and Train a WEIMARANER
How to Raise and Train a BASSET HOUND
How to Raise and Train a YORKSHIRE TERRIER

How to Raise and Train a Pedigreed or Mixed-Breed PUPPY
How to HOUSEBREAK and TRAIN YOUR DOG

ACKNOWLEDGMENTS

The photographs in this book were taken by Three Lions, Inc. and Louise Van der Meid with the cooperation of the best kennels in the world.

Contents

1. WHY TRAIN YOUR DOG? 5
   Let's Look at the Problem . . . When to Start Training . . . Do You Want
   an Alert-Looking Dog?

2. HOUSEBREAKING YOUR PUPPY 8
   Paper Training First . . . Working the Night Shift . . . The Real Training
   Begins . . . Curb Training

3. TRAINING YOUR DOG TO LIVE WITH HUMANS 16
   Teach Him to Stay by Himself . . . Curing the Barking Habit . . . Bones
   Are for Chewing . . . Jumping on People Isn't Polite . . . Keep off the
   Furniture . . . Chasing Cars May Be Fatal . . . Other Animals Are Off
   Limits Too . . . Training the Delinquent Dog . . . The Canine Crook
   and the Biter . . . Handling Your Puppy . . . Curing the Food-Stealer
   . . . Now Comes the Fun

4. OBEDIENCE TRAINING 29
   How Your Dog Learns . . . Your Voice Is Important . . . Set a Schedule
   . . . The First Goals in Obedience Training . . . The Proper Collar and
   Leash . . . Lesson One — For You . . . "Dog, Heeel" . . . Some Problems
   in Training to Heel . . . The Figure Eight . . . "Heel" Means Sit, Too
   . . . Sit and Stay . . . Come to Heel . . . If You Have a Big Dog . . .
   "Down, Dog!" . . . Stand on Command . . . Come on Command . . .
   Heeling Free

5. ADVANCED OBEDIENCE TRAINING 56
   Drop on Recall . . . Dumbbell Retrieving . . . First Step — "Hold It!" . . .
   Now, "Take It!" . . . Let's Carry It . . . Retrieving on Command . . .
   Jumping on Command . . . Retrieve Over Obstacle . . . The Broad Jump
   . . . The Long Sit and Down . . . Where Do You Go From Here? . . .
   Obedience Trials

6. TRAINING FOR FUN 73
   Begging . . . Shake Hands . . . Roll Over . . . Through the Hoop . . .
   Playing Dead . . . Speaking on Command

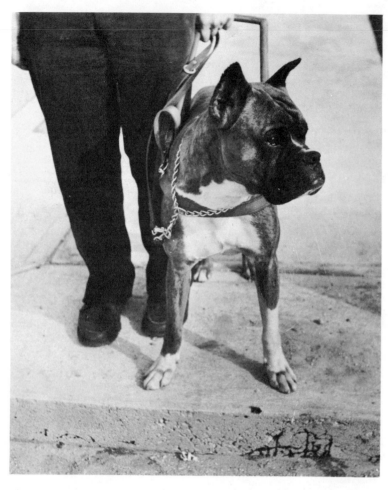

The peak of obedience training is shown in the work of the guide dog for the blind. You can apply the learning ability of your dog, training him to be a better companion, by following the principles of obedience training.

1. Why Train Your Dog?

The main purpose of dog training is to make your pet a better citizen. After all, your dog didn't ask to live in surroundings governed by rules made by and for humans. He'd probably be much happier roaming the woods like his wild ancestors, but with your help he can learn to live with humans — and like it.

In many ways, training a dog is like raising a child. You have to be firm, but kind, gentle, wise and above all persistent. Animal psychologists have never been able to explain it, but the dog is one animal that seems to have an instinctive desire to please the person who belongs to him. Most other animals are trained by fear, but the dog will do what you want him to — if you are able to get your message over to him despite the language barrier.

There are three basic schools of dog training. One tries to train by punishment and praise, another by rewards in the form of dog candies, and the third by demonstration, correction and praise. Training by fear will work on many dogs, but the end-product will be a dog that obeys unwillingly and loses much of the spirit that makes a dog such an enjoyable member of the family. Training by rewards will produce a spoiled dog that may perform tricks, but lacks the spirit of willing cooperation that marks the properly trained dog.

To help your dog grow into an animal that will be accepted by your neighbors as a law-abiding fellow citizen, use the proven method of demonstration, correction and praise described in this book. Show your dog what you want him to do, correct him if he makes mistakes, praise him to the skies when he does it correctly. That method has been used by the author of this book and scores of his friends who are members of the Suffolk Obedience Training Club of Long Island, and it is the method used by many of the owner-exhibitors who show their dogs in obedience contests and take home trophies and ribbons as recognition of the progress their dogs are making towards canine citizenship.

Actually, the purpose of a book on dog training is not to train the dog, but to train the dog's owner. If you were to attend an obedience training class, you would find that the instructor's words of criticism are not directed at the dogs, but at the person who is at the other end of the leash.

Let's Look At The Problem

First, don't expect your dog to understand the English language. You can shout, "I'll break your neck if you dirty the carpet!" It's plain to you what you mean, but to a puppy it's just a series of loud unpleasant sounds that may frighten him into another immediate violation of the rules of good behavior that have been set by humans for canines.

If you find that you cannot control your temper, let someone else take over the job of dog training. Training a dog calls for patience more than anything else. The same person who will allow a baby two years or more to learn the purpose of the functional apparatus in the bathroom expects a dog-baby to get the same basic idea in a few days.

No matter how clever your dog is, he can never learn to understand human language. After he has had enough contact with people he may learn to interpret your wishes through the tone of your voice and your hand motions. Remember always that the *sound,* not the *words,* is what the dog learns to understand.

Be consistent when you train your dog. Perhaps the most important first step is to build the number of words your dog understands. Limit your commands to as few words as possible, and always use the same words in the same order. For example, your dog will learn his name much more quickly if everyone calls him by the same name. Hearing "Junie," "Juniper," "Dog," and "hey, you!" at different times will drive the poor animal into a state of confusion. The call to "come and get it" should be one word, like "food" or "dinner." Announcing the meal as "breakfast," "lunch," "supper" or "your kibble and milk" will make his job of recognition that much harder.

Use affection as your best training tool. Every dog will respond to signs that he is liked and that his efforts to cooperate are appreciated. It may seem silly to you as a grown person to use baby talk to a dog, but the soft words of praise and affection will bring responsive behavior from dogs — even from the larger and "tougher" breeds.

When To Start Training

Housebreaking — which will be the first phase of training that we'll take up — can start as soon as the new puppy comes into your home, although if he is very young it will be some time before the training is successfully completed. When the puppy is old enough to walk, his training may begin. The first thing he should learn is a short command such as "No," or "Stop," which is his signal not to do whatever he may be doing at the time. He'll soon associate that word with something wrong. At the same time, familiarize him with the sound that means praise or permission, "good dog," or "okay."

From three to four months of age is the time to work on house manners and learning to walk on the leash. (Incidentally, "doggy" people never refer to this as the leash; they always say "lead.")

If you plan to go ahead with the more intensive training in obedience

6

routines that we'll cover in the second part of the book, you'll have to wait a while. For the average dog, such training should begin at the age of eight to ten months. Some dogs are more precocious and can begin serious work at about six months; others enjoy longer puppyhood and aren't ready to settle down to training until they're about a year old. Different breeds and different individual dogs will vary in this respect; the results you get as you begin training should be your clue to whether to go ahead or to slow down.

Do You Want An Alert-Looking Dog?

Chances are that you would like to have an alert-looking dog who carries his head high. One trick of the professionals is this: when you pet your puppy, resist the natural impulse to pat the top of his head. When you want to show affection, scratch him under the chin or play with the fur on his throat. Then when he wants to come over and be friends, he'll come over with his head held high. Head-patted dogs learn to carry their heads low to make head-patting easier; chin-scratched dogs hold theirs high. And now, to the first triumph of civilization over dog — housebreaking the puppy.

The main difference between an *animal* and a *pet* is training. It is up to you, the owner of the dog, to instruct your pet in the essentials of good behavior.

7

2. Housebreaking Your Puppy

First, face the grim fact that a puppy cannot be successfully housebroken until he is about four months old. If you are able to take him outdoors every two or three hours, he will be able to cooperate at a younger age, but the puppy under four months old is just too young to control himself physically for more than a few hours.

Usually the puppy that joins your family will be eight to ten weeks old. At that age, he's better off staying in the house, since there is the danger of picking up germs or worms on the outside, and the changes in temperature may be too drastic for him. Showing off a new puppy is a lot of fun, but it isn't really fair to the animal.

Paper Training First

There are two distinct steps in housebreaking the puppy. First, paper training, then the housebreaking itself. The best location for the new puppy is in the kitchen. There he's more likely to have company, and the smaller space of the kitchen makes it less likely that he will be subjected to the drafts that are found along the floors of larger rooms. At the start, spread several thicknesses of paper over the entire area that you set aside for the puppy, and barricade it so that he is limited to that area. For the coming weeks, that should be the puppy's daytime home. The main idea at this stage of the game is to keep the puppy from making any mistakes in a place where there are no papers.

Dogs are instinctively clean animals and will not foul the places where they sleep or play. Let that natural instinct help you in training your pet. After the first few days, your puppy will probably pick out a special corner to use as the men's or ladies' room. When you notice that sign of progress, praise him and then gradually reduce the area that's covered by paper. You can expect the puppy to make some mistakes now, and it's your job to show him that there is a definite connection between the paper and his business. When he makes an off-paper mistake, pick him up quickly and put him back on the paper. Scold him for his mistakes, but don't rub his nose in it or beat him. He'll try when he gets the right idea into his little head.

A partition across the doorway will provide a comfortable, satisfactory haven for your puppy while he is being housebroken. Training is much more difficult if he is allowed to roam through the house.

Watch your puppy carefully for signs that he's getting ready for action. Most dogs will act uneasy or run around in a short circle before doing anything. An older puppy will sniff the floor first, but one of the fastest acts in the animal world can be a puppy's quick squat. If you can reach him quickly enough, pick him up and put him on the paper, then use lavish words and petting to show what a smart and good dog he is. During the paper-training period, never leave the dog in a room where papers are not readily available to him.

A dog's life is lived in a world of smells. The dog's nose is as important to him as his eyes. You can make the training easier if you leave a piece of soiled paper on the floor when you clean up after him. That will help guide him back to the desired spot.

After a week or so of this routine, you'll probably be sorry you ever got a dog and will swear that the only pets you'll ever want again will be goldfish or caged birds. In addition, dogs relapse in their paper training. A puppy that's been a perfect little lady or gentleman will suddenly forget all about the reason for paper being on the floor, and you'll have to be patient and start the training routine all over again, but he'll learn. They all do.

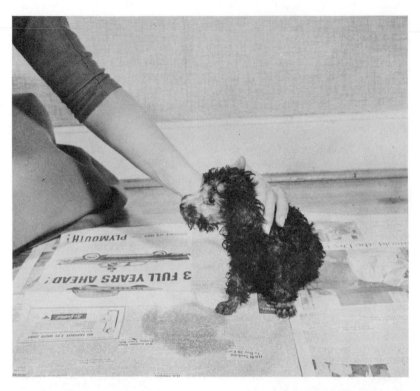

Use your puppy's natural instincts to make the job of housebreaking easier. Put a piece of soiled newspaper down, so that his nose will lead him to the spot he's expected to use.

Working The Night Shift

When your puppy approaches his fourth month, you can begin preparing him for housebreaking, if you are willing and able to give up a considerable part of your night's sleep. As we have mentioned, a puppy won't soil his sleeping quarters if he can help it. So, when you put him into his bed at night, tie him with a leash or piece of thin rope that's just long enough to let him roam around in his sleeping space, but not long enough to let him get outside that space. When he has to do anything, he'll whine or bark. That wakes you up. You take the puppy outside. That's a big step forward in his training and will speed up his housebreaking. However, if you'd rather sleep, you can leave him untied at night and hope that he'll use the papers. If he makes a nighttime mistake, don't try to correct him for it the next morning. To be effective, corrections must follow right on the heels of his mistake. A puppy who gets bawled out at eight o'clock in the morning for something that may have happened four hours earlier just doesn't connect the two events and doesn't understand why his owner is suddenly turning on him.

The Real Training Begins

At the age of four months, your puppy should be ready for the socially important housebreaking training. Here you must make a choice. If your dog will be left alone for long periods of time, you may want to combine housebreaking with paper training, and put papers down at night and when you leave the dog at home alone. If your goal is a completely housebroken dog, then remove all papers from the floor during the day. It may be advisable for a while to spread some papers at night for an emergency.

Don't expect your young dog to get the idea immediately, and don't give him the run of the house yet. When you let him out of his living quarters watch him carefully. At this time, an ounce of prevention is worth the proverbial pound of cure. Never let the puppy out of your sight. When you're eating keep his leash tied to the leg of your chair or under your foot. When he's playing and running free, keep a watchful eye on him. When you notice him sniffing the floor, or showing any other indications that he's getting ideas, use the word that he's associated with something naughty, pick him up and rush him outdoors — or to his paper. Don't scream at him or throw things.

This is the wrong approach. A piece of paper spread on the floor doesn't mean anything to the young puppy until he has been trained.

11

When your puppy begins to get the idea, cut down the paper-covered area. Soon he'll learn to use the corner of the room that's covered with paper. When he learns, praise him.

By now he's old enough to begin controlling his muscles and should be taught that some things must be done on schedule. To make it easier, take him out at the times that he would naturally have the urge. Take him out first thing in the morning, after every meal, after every period of excited or hard play, and the last thing at night. Be very careful not to confuse him. A mistake on your part can set the training back more than a dozen mistakes on his part can.

One puppy we knew was trying to become housebroken, so one afternoon he dashed out on the lawn and prepared to squat. An entire family screamed at him to get off the grass, so the poor thing became completely confused, ran back into the house and used the living room carpet. For days after that, he had the idea that the outdoors was taboo and that he had to use the carpet to please his people.

You are not being cruel to your puppy if you keep him confined to his barricaded room during most of his housebreaking period. He'll soon learn to "ask" to be let out when he has to do anything, and that's an important step in his development. In spite of all your precautions and your dog's efforts to cooperate, there are bound to be serious mistakes during the housebreaking period. You must control your temper. When a mistake happens, lead the dog over to the spot by his collar and explain in a severe tone of voice that such misconduct will not be tolerated. Your dog will generally show by his attitude that he realizes that he's the culprit. Try to make this correction immediately after the offense is committed. If you feel that you have to hit him — it may make you feel better — hold him firmly and give him a sharp slap on the hindquarters and then take him outdoors to fix in his mind that inside is bad, outside is good. Never chase him and try to slap him as he runs past you, or use a folded newspaper as your whipping strap unless you are holding him firmly at the time. If your dog is one of the large short-haired breeds, you will find that his body is very hard, and that the slap hurts your hand more than it does the animal.

At this early age puppies learn quickly, and if yours once manages to escape punishment by ducking and running away, you'll have a bit of a problem on your hands. To get back to canine psychology again, a puppy —or even a grown dog—does not seem to resent punishment if it's deserved. He won't hold it against you if he's caught in the act and disciplined immediately. You'll be amazed at how soon after a violent lecture from you, your dog will be back to apologize and make amends for his errors. But if he's punished some time later, he won't connect the act and the punishment.

If you find that your puppy seems to prefer certain spots that don't meet with your approval, you can buy sprays or liquids at the pet shop that will discourage him from visiting the areas you want to keep him from. The odors that keep the dog away are not offensive to humans.

Some puppies use anti-housebreaking tactics to show their resentment against people. They know that inside is not allowed, but when they're left alone or being trained in a manner that annoys them, they leave a puddle or deposit to show their resentment. Some will even choose the master's bed for this activity. If your dog does that, then you are permitted to lose your temper a little and let him know that such stunts will not be tolerated.

A regular routine will help your dog learn to be housebroken. Try as far as possible to feed him at regular hours and walk him on schedule. Set his last meal of the day at about 5 or 6 P.M. and give him very little liquid then.

It will take some time before your puppy learns just what part of the outside world he should head for, so it's a good idea to carry some paper towels in your pocket or purse to remove evidence of his public mistakes.

Curb Training

"Curb Your Dog" is a rule set by humans for dogs, and one that violates the dog's point of view. A dog would prefer to roam around, select a spot that pleases him, and take his own time about the matter. In addition, most dogs are modest creatures and when roaming loose will find an isolated spot. However, the city-living dog must be curb trained to avoid angry neighbors and the possibility of a visit to court by his owner.

When you first try to curb train your dog you will have your hands full. Perhaps the best way, if possible, is to combine curb training with house-breaking. When you lead or carry your puppy outside, set him down in the roadway and walk him back and forth in the curb until he leaves a puddle. Then, be lavish with praise. Allow yourself a lot of time for this process. It may take as long as a half-hour of walking and urging before anything happens. If you teach your dog some one word that he can associate with the act of using the curb, it will help. Use a word that he won't connect with any other training command. The writer used the command "Hurry" to train a Boxer in this performance, and he has been careful ever since not to use that same word in any other connection when directing that dog.

You have to be persistent now to get the idea of the curb fixed in your dog's mind. If nothing happens despite your urgings and the walking back and forth, take the puppy back into the house and tie him or put him in his box. Do not allow him to run free. Wait a while and try again. If still no luck, then bring him back and confine him again. Sooner or later he'll use the curb, and once it happens you've won a victory. For the next few times, take your puppy to the same place, then gradually accustom him to using other curb areas. You'll get quite a thrill of accomplishment the first time he rushes out to the curb by himself.

You'll remember that we suggested using a special code word for this business. With it, you can help the dog learn that there is a difference between walking for fun and going outside for business. In addition to your voice and hands, the leash is a means of communicating with your dog. When he is in the curb, hold the leash slack and walk around slowly. When you're walking for fun or exercise, hold the leash more tightly and walk along at a brisk pace. You can anticipate a few sidewalk mistakes, but they'll be fewer if you watch him carefully and snap back the leash and pull him to the curb at the first signs of a squat or determined sniffing at the sidewalk.

If you find that you are having a problem getting the idea across, it may help to take a piece of soiled newspaper and put it down in the road the first few times to help your puppy get the idea of what you expect of him. You're trying to get a whole new idea across. Before this, he was criticized every time he went off the newspaper; now he's being told to use the gutter, and he's naturally a little mixed up. To the dog, there isn't anything basically different between the floor of the living room and the street. Do all you can to make this intricate learning problem easier, and be certain to reward him with praise when he begins to get the idea. At the

Not every dog can be trained "to the pot." Take your dog out as frequently as possible . . .
and remember CURB YOUR DOG!

same time, you can become a bit firmer about your treatment of violations
in the home and elsewhere. A dog that's old enough to go out into the gutter
with the other dogs is old enough to accept responsibilities of community-
living with people.

In summarizing this business of paper training and housebreaking all
we can suggest is this: Ask yourself how old you were before you were
fully housebroken.

3. Training Your Dog to Live with Humans

As soon as your puppy has become fairly reliable in the matter of housebreaking, you can proceed with training him to be an acceptable member of your family and the community. The basic ingredients of training are these: your dog should stay at home by himself without making a fuss, his barking should be kept within limits, he shouldn't chew things, he shouldn't jump up on people, he shouldn't chase cars, cats or other dogs. By devoting a little time to your puppy you can help him grow into a desirable dog, and training him won't take the joy of dogdom out of his life. A trained dog is a happy dog. Dogs don't need canine delinquency to make them happy, and despite what owners of spoiled dogs tell you, training a dog, if it is done properly, will not affect his spirit or turn him into a fear-ridden robot.

Teach Him To Stay By Himself

No dog likes to be left home alone. Dogs can't read or enjoy TV. They get bored and they express their boredom by chewing up things in the house or indulging in a barking tantrum that will affect your relationship with your neighbors—and may break your lease if you live in an apartment house.

When the puppy comes into your home he may be noisy for the first few days and nights. Human babies spend the first part of their lives crying and puppies react in pretty much the same way. When your puppy is first shut up in his box or in the cut-off section of a room he will complain loudly. Provide him with some toys to keep him occupied. You might put a clock near him so that the ticking keeps him company. He will be cozy if he has an old blanket or rug to curl up in. In winter a hot water bottle will help replace the warmth of his littermates.

After the first couple of days, begin showing your puppy that barking noises aren't approved of. Use the words "No!" or "Stop!" with emphasis and combine them with an angry finger waved at the puppy's nose. Above all, don't let your children or neighbors praise the puppy for barking. Just one word of admiration for a puppy's bark can ruin a week of no-bark training.

When you first leave the puppy at home alone, don't give him the free run of the house. Allowing a young dog the freedom of an empty house is an open invitation to repair bills. It is also unwise to tie the puppy's leash to a piece of furniture or radiator when you leave him. Many puppies have strangled themselves in an effort to get rid of the leash; others try to free themselves by chewing anything within reach. Make it easier for your puppy by leaving him in an enclosed area with which he is familiar, and with some familiar toys.

Begin the leave-alone training by leaving the dog in one room with the door closed, while you go into another room. As soon as you hear the beginnings of a bark, command "Quiet," or shout "Stop," or "No." If the barking continues, pound sharply on the door and command him to stop. If that doesn't work, open the door, take him by the collar and show him who's boss. This phase of the training will often turn into a contest with the dog and you trying to outsmart each other.

Often the puppy will keep quiet if he thinks someone is in the house with him, but when he thinks he's alone, he begins to exercise his vocal cords. To counter that, walk to the outside door, open it, slam it, and then sneak back into your home. At the first bark shout loudly at your puppy or hit the door with the palm of your hand. The pup will be so surprised that he'll forget about barking. Another way is to remain near your front door until you hear barking, then pound on the door or go inside for a discussion of the situation with your dog.

As soon as your puppy decides that barking when alone only gets him into trouble, he'll stop. However, there's a word of caution. Some breeds of dogs bark more than others. As a rule of thumb, the smaller the dog, the more likely he is to be a barker when left alone. That means that you'll have to work harder on this problem if your puppy is one of the smaller, yappier breeds.

As for chewing, handle that like any other violation. Collar your puppy, bring him face to face with the chewed object, and explain loudly and firmly that chewing is no way to endear himself to you. Then banish him to a corner or to his bed, but give him his chewing toy so that he'll get the idea that there are chewables and unchewables in this world of humans and dogs.

Curing The Barking Habit

Have you ever tried to give up smoking? You probably found that you had to give it up completely or give in to it. It's the same with your dog's barking. It's natural for dogs to bark—except the Basenjis who can't bark, and the Samoyeds who would rather make their own howling sound.

If you want your dog to be a watchdog, then let him bark. If you are living in an apartment house or for other reasons prefer a non-barker, you can train your dog not to bark. If you start with a puppy and cut him short

17

every time he begins to bark, he will grow into a quieter dog. If you acquire an older dog that has the barking habit, it may take more time, but he can learn, too. When you are walking your dog and he barks, pull him back sharply with the leash and tell him to be quiet. Indoors, grab him by the nose, place your hands around his muzzle and hold tight till he gives up the idea of barking. If he persists, get a necktie and wrap the middle around the dog's muzzle and tie the ends around his neck. That sounds complicated, but if you try, you'll find it possible. Leaving that on for a few minutes won't hurt the dog, but it will make it impossible for him to bark and after a while he'll get the idea.

Another technique is to make something unpleasant happen every time the dog barks. Slam down a book or folded newspaper. Hit a table with a strap to make a loud noise. Most dogs dislike noise and as soon as yours realizes that the barking brings on the other unpleasant noise, he'll cut down on his barking.

Some dogs just don't like to be tied up. If they are tied to anything, they'll bark, but they'll stop as soon as they're freed. If that's the case with your dog, then don't tie him. The dogs that complain if they are tied will not bark if they are in a confined area just so long as they are not tied down.

For the dog's sake be consistent. Don't say "good dog" one time he barks and try to discipline him for the same act another time. Once you have eliminated unwanted barking, you can still teach your dog to bark on command or to ask for things. If the dog wants anything, he can make other sounds that are loud enough to attract your attention without barking. It's a compliment to your dog and your training when the neighbors ask "Can your dog bark? I never heard him." That can be accomplished with consistent effort on your part.

Bones Are For Chewing

Dogs chew things. That's part of a dog's way of life, and if your dog could talk, he'd find some faults with you. Until your puppy is at least six months old, there isn't much you can do about the chewing problem. After he's learned the word "No," he can be stopped before he chews specific things, if you catch him in time. Some dog owners seem to get a perverse pride in telling about the valuable things their young dogs have managed to chew up. However, by constantly disciplining your dog when he chews things that shouldn't be chewed and by playing with him and directing his attention to approved chewables, you can reduce the damage to your possessions.

If you buy a dog bed, avoid the wicker type because young dogs enjoy chewing them to pieces. Buy your puppy some hard rubber toys and the treated bones that won't splinter when he gnaws on them. Avoid soft rubber playthings—chewed-up pieces of rubber can cause serious internal trouble to a puppy—or an older dog. Your puppy will probably want to chew on

Keeping your puppy in a wicker basket may be dangerous if the dog chews up the wood. Wait until the puppy is over six months old before using anything but a metal bed.

pieces of wood, but try to discourage that because the splinters may be swallowed with consequent bad effects.

There is disagreement in the dog world — among the people, that is — as to why dogs chew. Some blame it on teething, others say they do it out of boredom, others that it's done to show resentment at being left alone.

When you train your dog to stay alone, treat the chewing problem along with the barking problem. And again, don't confuse the dog. Letting him chew one slipper and spanking him if he chews another is most confusing. Try to teach him that the things he may chew are very different from the things he may not chew. When you bring him a chewing toy, introduce him to it, play with it, hold it while he chews it, praise him for being a smart puppy. When he gets a little older, increase the severity of his corrections for chewing offenses. An adult dog will often chew things out of spite. That's willful misconduct and calls for a spanking and banishment to a lonely corner where he can ponder his sins.

Above all, don't let a kindly member of your family interfere with chewing discipline. That person would be the first to wail if her possessions (it's usually a female member of the family) were destroyed by the animal.

The best method of training your dog not to jump on people is to bend your leg when he jumps and knock him over. He will only take this bouncing once or twice before he learns not to jump.

Jumping On People Isn't Polite

Dogs naturally like people. One way they show affection is by jumping up on people. That's good for the cleaning business, but sometimes the recipient doesn't appreciate paw marks across the front of a new dress or suit, and many people are afraid of dogs or can just tolerate them. Having a large dog knock him off balance may even prejudice a dog-lover against your animal.

By the time your puppy is four months old, you can begin to teach him that people are not to be jumped on. When he does it, shout "No" and push him down firmly. Be consistent. Correct him every time he jumps on a person, even on family members and close friends. It's hard for him to give up a habit that's fun unless he's stopped every time he does it.

There are several ways of curing an older dog of people-jumping. One calls for a bit of agility on your part. When the dog jumps up, step firmly on one of his back paws. After that happens a few times, the dog will decide that jumping isn't worth a couple of pinched toes and he'll stop.

The other way is to send the dog reeling back when he jumps up on anyone. You can lift your knee just as the dog jumps and knock him backwards. It won't hurt him, but the unexpected collision will jar him, and if this is combined with a verbal correction, he'll get the idea. However, call him over immediately afterward and pet him, so that he won't think the human race has suddenly turned against him.

A less acrobatic way is to grab the dog's front paws when he jumps up, throwing him down backwards. Any of these corrections should be accompanied by a harsh word so that the dog won't think it's some new kind of game, and followed by a friendly word immediately afterward. As your dog advances in training and learns the meaning of "Sit," he can be commanded to sit when anyone approaches, and to say "hello" without getting overexcited.

Keep Off The Furniture

The average dog finds jumping on furniture almost as satisfactory as jumping on people. The dog should have his own bed, but very few dogs can resist the temptation to try the couches or sofas. Your dog may look very charming sitting on your sofa, but once he becomes a furniture-hopper he thinks he belongs on furniture. What happens if you buy new furniture or if you take him visiting? Furniture is comfortable for a dog and once your puppy has tried it you have a problem. So chase him down with a firm "No" and continue to enforce the "no dog on furniture" rule.

If your dog already has the furniture-climbing habit, it calls for sterner measures. A dog that keeps off the furniture when you are home may climb aboard as soon as the front door closes. Complaining to him when you get home won't be very effective. One old trick to combat this is to place a small mouse trap, set but without cheese, on the piece of furniture that the dog patronizes. Once he finds that the furniture bites at him and makes a sharp noise, he will be cured of his liking for furniture. If you're afraid the trap will hurt him—a small one won't—you can get a similar effect by spreading crinkly, noisy cellophane on the furniture, or by using some child's toy that lets out a squawk when touched.

Sometimes the dog isn't to blame for his furniture-climbing habits. If your dog persists, check his sleeping quarters to make sure that there isn't a draft when a door or window is open.

Chasing Cars May Be Fatal

According to figures gathered by a dog research organization, more dogs die from automobile accidents than from any other single cause. Strangely,

Chasing automobiles can be a fatal pastime. If your dog is developing that habit, make the cure for it the first thing on your training schedule.

That spot on the upholstered chair is more comfortable than his own sleeping-place, but he must learn that furniture is for people. Scold him severely and use a dog-repellent or the mousetrap trick if he persists in using your furniture.

some dogs become automobile chasers, others do not. If yours develops that dangerous habit, it calls for severe action on your part. First, train your dog to keep off the road, except when the line of duty requires him to use the gutter near the curb.

A dog that runs free in the country will probably have some narrow escapes that will teach him respect for a car, but the animal that spends his outdoor time on a leash doesn't have the opportunity to learn such respect for a moving car. Whether the dog you are training is a city- or country-dweller, he should be firmly taught that cars and dogs do not mix.

Training a dog to have car-respect can be done if you have the cooperation of a driver for the car. Walk down the road with the dog, with the car approaching slowly from the rear. When the car is a few feet away, the driver should blast the horn loudly. At the same time you pull the dog off the side of the road and let the car pass. After repeating that lesson a few times, the dog should start to look back over his shoulder when he hears a car coming and move over to the side of the road without any urging. When that happens, praise him. If it doesn't happen, jerk the leash hard enough to pull him off the road. Repeat when needed.

For confirmed car-chasing dogs, the cure is to associate something unpleasant with the act of car-chasing. There are many different things that can be done. The driver of the car can squirt your dog with a water pistol. If you can find a long carriage whip, a few flicks on a dog's side will convince him that car-chasing only means trouble. A more tractable dog will be cured if the car stops and the driver yells at him or chases him. The correction should be drastic enough to make the dog turn tail and run — and remember the incident.

Teaching a dog that car-chasing isn't done will not prejudice him against cars in general. He'll still be as anxious as ever for his rides in the family auto.

There's one note of caution in training against car-chasing. Some dogs become so excited when they chase a car that they may try to attack the person who comes out of the car to correct them. The owner should always be close at hand to step in if this happens and to take prompt action to prevent any biting.

Other Animals Are Off Limits Too

Some breeds of dogs are more likely to chase cats and other dogs. General obedience training will help you control your dog, but if he breaks away and gets close to a cat the chances are he'll regret it. If your dog shows signs of becoming a runner-away, walk him on a long line — about 15 or 20 feet long — firmly attached to his collar. When he gets to the end of the line, give it as hard a yank as you can — it won't hurt your dog, whose neck is strong — and pull him back with a lecture on the undesirability of such actions.

A dog that is well trained to stay within his permitted area outdoors will present less of a chasing or running-away problem. Even a fairly young puppy can be taught the limits of his territory. Walk him around the area in which he is expected to stay. Point outside with a firm "No." Anytime he wanders off, call or pull him back with a stern reprimand, and soon he'll recognize his boundaries and stay within them.

Some trainers recommend slinging shots off the dog's flanks with a BB gun, or bombarding him with pebbles and clods of dirt when he attempts to wander off limits, but verbal persuasion and a limited amount of discipline should provide the same results with less effect on the dog's nervous system.

Training The Delinquent Dog

There are delinquents in the dog world and they present as much of a problem as our more-publicized human juvenile delinquents. If your young

Don't allow begging at the table. A firm command will put a stop to that and let you enjoy your meal in peace. If your dog persists, out of the room for him!

dog shows traces of a vicious temperament and doesn't outgrow it by the time he's six months old, you should give serious thought to getting rid of him, or turning him over to a professional dog trainer who may be able to straighten him out for you. Viciousness in a dog is most often the result of improper breeding, and the kennel or pet shop that sold you the dog should be responsible and should give you another dog in exchange.

Very young puppies often growl and snap in infantile fits of anger. This should not be regarded as amusing. Let the puppy know that you do not permit such behavior. Constant teasing of a puppy can easily lead to trouble later on. Don't grab away your dog's toys and bones, even in play. Don't encourage a young puppy and young children to play tug-of-war because this game will teach a puppy the power of his teeth too soon.

When your puppy is eating, make it a habit to feed him a few bites of his meal by hand so that he won't resent a person who approaches him at mealtime. If you have more than one puppy, feed them separately so that they won't have to growl and chase other dogs away when they're eating.

The Canine Crook And The Biter

Some dogs develop a habit of taking things and then trying to bite anyone who attempts to take the object away from them. The dog that grabs a stocking or piece of clothing and refuses to give it up without an argument is just reflecting a lack of training.

If your dog shows resentment and refuses to give up something he is holding, you must act promptly and firmly to avoid future trouble. Take hold of whatever he is holding and firmly command him to "Drop it!" or say "Out." If he lets go, then take it calmly and praise the dog. If it's something he should have, give it back to him. If it's something he shouldn't have, then put it down and play with the dog to get his mind off it.

When the dog refuses to give it up, or growls or snaps, don't grab for the object or you'll probably be bitten. If the dog is small enough for you to handle, and if he is wearing a collar, pick him up by the collar with one hand. When he begins choking take the object out of his mouth quickly. If the dog is too large for that, try slapping him quickly on the nose to make him drop the object. Very often the dog is bluffing and a show of firmness on your part will make him back down. If you are bitten — and it can happen in such a situation — you'll have to decide whether to put up with that kind of behavior in the future, or to take drastic action.

A pair of heavy gloves may enable you to force the dog's mouth open, take out the object and administer the deserved punishment — which is fully merited by his behavior. Bribing the dog to surrender the object is only building up a nasty trait in his character.

Handling a dog that is trying to bite you is dangerous. With an angry small dog, hoisting him up into the air and holding him by his collar may cool him off. Lower him to the ground when he seems to calm down. If he still tries to bite, hoist him up again. The choking and discomfort may teach him that trying to bite people isn't a good idea. To lift an angry dog from the floor, hold the leash in your right hand, pull it forward and keep it tight. Then lift the dog up quickly with your left hand. If you keep the leash tight as you pick up the dog, he can't bring his head around to grab your hand. But make certain that the collar is tight enough so that the dog can't pull his head through it and escape.

If you're afraid to handle your dog when he gets angry, a fast well-placed kick, hard enough to send him flying, may serve to solve the immediate problem. But the dog that wants to bite humans is a danger in the home and outside.

Handling Your Puppy

Some dogs won't let their owners or anyone else brush or comb them. That seldom happens if the puppy becomes accustomed to being handled. Examine your puppy's eyes and ears daily. When you examine him, run your hands over every part of his body, especially underneath and around the tail. Open his mouth and run your fingers over his teeth. At any sign of resentment, give him a sharp slap on the hindquarters and tell him to behave. If he always growls or tries to snap when you touch a particular part of his body, have the vet look at him. There may be an injury or weakness that causes pain when he is touched, and it should be corrected. As you

Your puppy will not mind being handled, even by strangers, if you get him used to it from an early age.

will see later, allowing himself to be examined by a stranger is one mark of the well-trained dog, and the dog that won't let himself be touched is going to be a problem on his visits to the vet.

Curing The Food-Stealer

Many dogs that are well fed at home will try to steal food from the garbage pail or other places and they view their outside walks as foraging expeditions. The same principles of training that you use in other phases of "bringing up Hector" should be used to curb this habit. However, this food-stealing busines can be prevented much more easily than it can be cured.

The instant your dog reaches for anything that he shouldn't have, he should hear a loud "No!" supplemented, if necessary, by a sharp slap on the nose. As in other training phases, it will help if you catch the culprit in the act and correct him immediately.

You can set up your own "crime scene" to be sure you catch him in the act. Leave pieces of food in different places around the room and keep a watchful eye on him. When he approaches one, order him away. If his conduct doesn't improve, become increasingly severe in your corrections.

If the dog attempts to pick food from the street while you have him on leash, a sharp jerk on the leash should put that idea out of his head. If you find that you have a problem child on your hands you might try one of the more drastic treatments. Have someone else — not you — prepare a small piece of meat with a liberal dosing of pepper and put it down where the dog will find it. One or two samples like that may convince him to stick to home cooking. Or, you might get out the old mousetrap and cover it with a cloth so that it won't catch your dog's tongue, and put a piece of meat on the cloth. The result when your dog goes for the meat should teach him a good lesson.

Now Comes The Fun

At this stage of dog training, it's probably true that you're wondering why you ever got a dog. All you've been doing is working to take a wild animal and try to turn him into a civilized member of the family. You've cleaned up his dirt, you've walked him in the rain and the cold, you've lost sleep and probably pounds. You've finally achieved the state of making your dog unobjectionable. But where's the fun in dog-owning? That comes next, with obedience training.

4. Obedience Training

Now your dog is six or eight months old. Let's hope that he's absorbed his puppy training and is a well-behaved member of the family. It really doesn't matter whether you have a purebred dog that you hope to enter in obedience shows, or just a plain, lovable dog. Obedience training makes a better and a happier dog. People who have never trained their dogs will excuse their neglect on the grounds that training ruins a dog's spirit. They say they'd rather have a dog with "personality" than a trained dog. If "personality" to you means a dog that has to be chased when you want him, a dog that pulls your arm out of your socket when you walk him (even a small dog can pull a leash awfully hard), a dog that won't associate socially with other dogs and with people, then don't bother training your dog — just let him grow up in his own way.

Dogs actually seem to enjoy being trained. While it's hard to read a dog's mind, trained dogs appear to get more out of life because training gives them something to do. Most dogs seem eager to get out for their "lessons." When you and your dog have mastered a new phase of training, the dog seems to be as happy with his accomplishment as you are. And most dogs appear to enjoy showing off their obedience work.

How Your Dog Learns

The basic method of obedience training is the same as puppy training. Your dog will learn by associating his acts with pleasant results. He finds that doing certain things earns him praise; doing other things brings him stern corrections. After a while the acts that have brought him praise become automatic and he learns to respond to voice, leash or hand signals and to do what is asked of him.

Training techniques vary slightly according to the breed of the dog and the personality of the handler, but these are the basic steps:

1. Your voice commands obedience.

2. You apply pressure on the leash to teach the dog what you want him to do.

3. Any incorrect response is immediately corrected.

4. A correct response is praised and repeated.

If your dog misbehaves during a training session, sit him down and have a heart-to-heart talk with him. Dogs know when they have done something wrong, and verbal correction is an important part of obedience training.

Your Voice Is Important

In puppy training, we recommended a firm control over your temper. This is even more important in obedience training. Drill sergeant techniques will seldom work on dogs. When you start training your dog, and every time you begin working on a new exercise, use a *coaxing,* baby-talk tone of voice to give the dog confidence and to make him want to perform the exercise. When he begins to get the idea, then give your commands in a loud, normal tone of voice. When he "goofs," reprimand him in a firm, stern tone of voice, but don't scream at him or throw things. While we don't want to enter the battle of the sexes, it is claimed that men are better dog trainers than women because they give their commands in a firmer tone of voice and with more authority, which the dog recognizes.

Set A Schedule

If possible, try to keep a training schedule for yourself and your dog. In the beginning, don't work with your dog for more than ten minutes at a time; as the training progresses, you can stretch the training sessions to a half-hour. Don't train your dog right after he has eaten. If you do, he'll probably get excited and throw up his latest meal. During the first sessions of a dog-training school, several of the dogs invariably deposit their half-digested food on the floor. Before you start a lesson take your dog out for a short walk so that his insides will be comfortable during "school." It's asking a lot, but for best results your training lessons should be held every day.

Seek distractions. It may be easier to train your dog where there are no distractions, but he should learn that obedience commands must be obeyed under any conditions. One advantage of attending an obedience school is that the dog learns in the company of other dogs and people. If possible, train your dog where he will see and hear other dogs. If you can't get a dog-place, children provide a good substitute. If you have none of your own, neighborhood kids will provide a willing and often noisy audience for your training sessions. Have other members of your family around while you are training your dog, and from the start make it clear to him that his attention must be kept on the person who is handling him. Let other members of the family take turns training and working with the dog. That may lead to plenty of family arguments about methods and results, but it will be good for the dog.

Train your dog where there are distractions. This Boxer would like to take off and play with the puppy, but his training is showing results. He's staying in his sit position without budging.

The First Goals In Obedience Training

The first goals in obedience training are to get your dog to walk along with you like a little gentleman or lady, staying at your left side or "heeling"; to sit, stay and lie down on command; to come at your call or signal. Actually that is the basis of the "Novice" obedience routine in obedience shows conducted by the A.S.P.C.A. and the various dog shows that are held under American Kennel Club rules. Learning these routines will qualify your dog for canine citizenship.

The Proper Collar and Leash

The training collar is a "must" for obedience training. This is the type of collar called a "chain slip collar," made of metal links with a ring at each

Study this picture carefully. It shows the correct way to put the "choke" collar on your dog. Trying to train a dog with a plain leather collar just won't work. Use of the "spike" collar is cruel and unnecessary.

Handle your dog regularly so that he won't become shy of people. That will make your trips to the vet or the dog-groomer a lot more pleasant, and it is a step towards his obedience training.

end. The right size for your dog will slip over his head easily with a four-inch or so overlap when the collar is on. When you buy one, get one with larger links in preference to a lightweight chain. You'll be jerking on the leash to give your dog commands and corrections and the heavier chain will be less likely to hurt the dog or cut his neck hair than a thin chain.

The other item is a training leash. This should be about six feet long, with a strong metal snap. The army surplus types made of strong webbed cloth are about the best for training use. A round leather leash is liable to slip through your hands and you'll find a chain leash impractical for training as the metal will cut your fingers when the dog acts up — as he will.

The ordinary three-foot leash or the shorter "traffic" leash are useless for training, as you'll find out if you try to use them.

Lesson One — For You

The first thing to learn about obedience training is how to put on the chain collar. The purpose of this collar is to tighten up when you pull on the leash, loosen when you release the pull. To get that effect, sit your dog at your left side. Slide the chain around his neck so that you can attach the leash to the ring at the end of the chain which passes *over*, not under his

Notice how the trainer is holding the leash in his right hand, with his left hand ready to take the leash, if necessary, and administer a sharp jerk for correction.

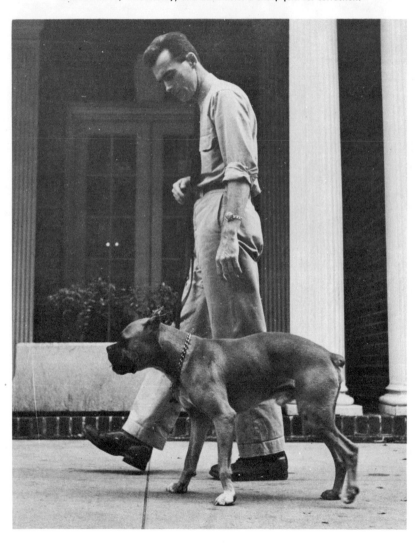

That's right, step out with a fast stride and long steps. Teaching your dog to heel is easier if you get in the habit of walking at a fast clip when you are training him.

neck. Study the illustration on page 32 showing the right way to put on the chain collar. Test it by pulling on the leash. The collar should tighten when you pull, slack off when you release.

With the dog at one end of the leash, and you at the other, you're ready. At the beginning, even with a small dog, training is a two-handed job. Hold the end of the leash in your right hand, in front of your body about waist high. Fold up the extra part of the leash so that you can hold it comfortably. If your dog is large or strong, put your hand through the loop in the leash so that you won't lose him if he decides he doesn't like the first lesson and tries to take off.

Place your left hand on the leash a bit above the dog's collar, and use that hand for corrections and to pat the dog when he does well. Later on, as you both progress, you'll be able to drop your left hand and control the leash with your right.

(Above) Make obedience training easier for your dog by giving him hand signals as well as verbal commands. This is the "stay" signal.

(Opposite page, top) If your dog pulls ahead of you, jerk back on the leash and set him in heel position. Use the word "heel" constantly while you are training your dog. He'll learn to connect the sound with what you expect of him.

(Opposite page, bottom) This is a good "sit" in the heel position. Note that the dog is sitting squarely with his head near his trainer's left knee.

37

This girl is pulling the dog rather than guiding him, but it's a good idea to let your children gain experience handling the dog even while he is learning his obedience routines. Many dogs will respond more quickly to children than to adults.

"Dog, HEEEL"

Now, take a deep breath and start off walking briskly. As you step off say your dog's name and the word "Heel." Stretch out the word with a long "ee" sound to help your dog make the connection between the word and what's expected of him. Step out with your left foot first as that's the one nearest the dog and he'll get the habit of watching that foot for his guidance.

Walk fast enough so that the leash keeps the dog moving at a brisk pace. Talk to the dog constantly, using the word "heel" frequently. Try to keep the dog near your left knee. Don't pull the leash, but rather try to keep the dog at your left knee by jerking him forward when he lags behind, pulling him back if he goes ahead.

The mistake most beginners make is walking too slowly. Walk as fast as you can during the first "heeling" sessions. Vary your direction. Don't be afraid of hurting the dog's neck with your corrections. If your dog isn't cooperating, jerk the leash hard enough to pull him off his feet. Be careful to jerk the leash in the direction you want him to walk, not up into the air. One good trick is to reverse your course, especially if your dog is lunging ahead. Make a sharp about-turn and jerk your dog after you, take a few quick steps and then reverse again. Try walking in a big circle, first to the left, then to the right. Make sharp turns to the right and to the left.

Make the dog understand that the command "heel" means that he must stay on your left side, close to you. When the dog is heeling properly, be lavish with your praise and tell him what a good dog he is. However, when your dog hears a word of praise during his first lessons, he may want to jump up and play or lick you. That calls for a verbal correction and a quick return to fast walking.

Some Problems In Training To Heel

Your dog may at first think his lesson is a new kind of game and he will try to introduce a variation by jumping up and trying to grab at your arm or hand. A stern "no" and increasing your speed to get the dog's mind back to business should take care of that nonsense.

If your dog tries to attack other dogs or starts to bark at them, jerk the lead hard and start off briskly in the opposite direction. If he gets too keyed up to pay any attention to you, you can rap him on the nose with the end of the leash.

A few dogs, even though they have become accustomed to walking on leash, will resent being taught to heel and will express this resentment by trying to bite their handlers. If your pet does this, just lift him up by the leash and hold him away from you at arm's length with his front paws in the air, until he cools off. You may find it easier to control a larger dog if you walk around in a small circle while holding him up. At this time, you have to show him who's boss. When you put him down, pat him and start heeling again. If he acts up again, back into the air for him until he realizes that it's either heel or choke. Remember that the faster you walk when you're teaching your dog to heel, the easier it will be for him to learn.

Try sharp left and right turns as soon as your dog begins to get the heeling idea fixed in his mind. On the turn to the right use a sharp jerk on the leash to get your dog started on his change of direction. On the left turn, you'll be turning into the dog's line of direction. As you turn sharply the first few times, you may find it necessary to lift your right knee into the dog's neck or chest to get him out of your way, if he's a big dog. A smaller dog can be pushed aside with the inside of your right foot. If you make your first left turns when your dog is slightly ahead of you, it may be harder and there may be some stumbling on your part, but it will help teach the dog that the proper heeling position is next to your left knee, not ahead of it.

Don't try too much too quickly in teaching heeling. Allow at least a week for your dog to get the basic idea fixed in his head.

Let's review the basic steps in this important first part of obedience training:

1. Make sure the collar is on correctly.
2. Keep the leash slack except when making corrections.
3. Jerk — do not pull the leash for corrections.
4. Keep on talking to your dog when you are working with him. Stress the word "heel."
5. Walk fast.
6. Change your speed and direction to keep the dog's interest up.
7. Be firm.
8. Limit first lessons to 10 minutes.

And above all, try to make the training fun for your dog and yourself. Play with your dog after a lesson, praise him when he does something well. Try to end each lesson on a pleasant note. Even if your dog has given you a hard time and refused to learn anything, go back to something he can do so that the session will end with praise. Take him for a relaxing fun-walk after each lesson.

The Figure Eight

Set two objects about eight feet apart. Walk between them and then execute a "figure eight" around them. When you first do this, circle to the left as that makes it easier for the dog. Your body is away from the object he is circling and this helps keep him in place. If he wanders or tries to pass on the wrong side, jerk him back with your leash.

When you circle to the right, with your dog on the outside, take shorter steps so that he doesn't get ahead of you. When you circle to the left, take longer steps so that he will not have to change his rate of speed to keep up with you.

Later, try this same maneuver around two people who are standing eight feet apart. This training for the Figure Eight routine, which is required in obedience shows, will train your dog to keep close to you when passing people, other dogs or any stationary objects.

"Heel" Means Sit, Too

Until now, you have been using the word "heel" as a command to your dog to walk at your left side. To make things a bit more confusing, the word "heel" is also the command for your dog to sit at the heel position.

Chances are that your dog has already learned the word "sit." As the second part of his obedience training, he must be taught to come to a sitting position at your left side, whenever you halt, without any command. Teaching your dog that is much simpler than it seems.

During your heeling practice, sit your dog whenever you come to a halt. First just try using the word "sit." If your dog responds to that, say "sit"

To teach your dog to heel beside you on leash, instead of dragging ahead or lagging, snap him forward.

every time you halt. Soon he'll get the idea and sit without any oral command. More often, however, it will take some training to achieve this. As you come to a halt, shorten the leash in your right hand. At the moment you stop, pull upwards with the leash, and at the same time push down on the hindquarters of your dog with your left hand.

The proper sitting position for the dog is squarely on both hips with head near your left knee. If you find that your dog is sitting at an angle or ahead of you, don't try to pull him to you — that will only confuse him. Jerk the leash, take a step or two forward, and get him down in the proper position.

Keep the dog sitting until you command him to move. If he tries to lie down, jerk him up with the leash and reprimand him. If he tries to stand up, push his hindquarters down again and repeat "sit." In teaching the dog to sit, try to avoid the use of his name with the command. At this stage of his training, when the dog hears his name it still means action and he'll automatically rise in response to it.

After you have been over this sitting business with your dog, force him down without any words each time you stop, until he understands what's expected of him. For some reason, this is one thing that dogs learn most easily. Your part is to get him to sit correctly.

Your dog may try to use you for a leaning post. If he does, a few bangs

Want him to sit? Use the verbal command "sit." At the same time, pull up on the leash and force his rear end down with your left hand. Soon he'll get the idea.

with your left leg should discourage that. It's the larger breeds that are most likely to try to lean against their trainer, and having a Great Dane resting on your left leg isn't too comfortable.

If your dog gets into the habit of sitting too far ahead, just put out your left foot when you come to a stop and jerk back on the leash. If he swings his rear end outward, lean over and slap his left thigh as he is coming down.

Be sure that you don't step on your dog's feet when you stop. That's painful and can set your training back as he'll try to sit far enough away to avoid your clumsiness once it happens.

Should he still sit too far away, try heeling him alongside a wall or in a narrow hallway where he just won't have room enough to sit too far from you.

As soon as your dog consistently sits whenever you stop, begin working on fixing the word "heel" in his mind as meaning to sit by your left side. Walk, stop, say "heel," praise your dog. Just take one or two steps, use the dog's name and the command "heel." Tell him how smart he is for learning that.

If you're a beginning trainer, it may be hard for you to tell whether the dog is sitting properly while you are standing alongside him, so have someone else watch him sit to see if he's straight, and correct any faults.

It's important to train your dog to come to you when you stop. It's natural to want to help your dog, and in almost every dog training class the beginning trainers will step closer to their dogs, or step backward if the dog is sitting behind them. That only gets the dog confused. And don't slap your own thigh and say "come on, dog, move closer." Remember, dogs don't understand words, just sounds — not even your own smart pooch.

Sit and Stay

As soon as you are reasonably sure that your dog understands the meaning of "heel" as a command to sit by your left side, test him by sitting down in a chair and telling him to heel. If that works then he's learned it and you should promote him to the next lesson, the "sit and stay." What you will try now is to teach your dog to stay on command in a sitting position.

Sit the dog on your left side and hold the leash in your right hand, loosely. Put your left hand around your dog's muzzle and step forward (with the right foot) until you're facing your dog. Keep him in a sitting position. Use the word "stay." Do not use the dog's name in this command, or in any command where the dog is to be left. If your dog makes any move, snap up the leash. If necessary, push his rear end down and repeat "stay." After a few seconds, go back to heel position, not circling the dog, and be careful not to jerk the leash. Then, start away from the dog again. This time, hold your left hand, palm back, in front of the dog's nose, and leave him, starting off with the right foot. Walk a few feet in front of him and stand facing him, ready to correct him if he starts to move, rise or lie down. Walk to the end of your leash. If your dog stays, walk back to heel position, circling him. If you notice that he's getting ready to move, give him a prompt correction. In teaching the sit and stay, move very slowly, except when making a correction. Do not praise the dog as a word of praise or a pat now will give him the idea that the exercise is over and send him bounding up.

Use the word "stay" as a correction only, saying it loudly when the dog threatens to move his position or stand up.

Next try putting the leash on the floor in front of the dog when he is in a sitting position. If he is still unsteady, keep your foot on the end of the leash.

Then, try walking behind your dog when he's sitting. If he breaks—and he probably will—don't correct him from a distance, and don't get him excited by running after him and slapping at him. Take him by the collar and firmly but gently bring him back to the place where he had been sitting. Sit him down and make him stay by standing in front of him.

Gradually increase the distance you wander away from him, and introduce distractions to fix the idea that "stay" means stay. Bounce balls around him, bring around other dogs or children, clap your hands, make noises, play a radio, even eat a piece of candy while he is staying—but make him stay.

This is the first exercise in which the dog is learning to do something while he is not being held by the leash and it is an important step in his development. Sometimes it may be helpful to have another person standing behind the dog to give a prompt correction.

When the dog stays while you are visible, step out of sight for longer and longer intervals. A properly trained dog should sit without moving—with his master out of sight — for five minutes or more. In obedience trials, the dogs in the second advanced stage of training must do this in the show ring for three minutes.

As you will see later, the sit-stay is the basis of several of the more advanced obedience routines and the dog that does not stay cannot learn the

When you leave your dog on a "stay" signal, be careful to step away with your right foot first. This routine is the basis of much of the advanced obedience training.

After receiving the command to stay, your dog should wait until you call him or return to him.

other required routines. All it takes is firmness and patience on your part. The fact that your dog gets up and follows you when you leave him does not necessarily mean that he loves you more than the other dogs love their owners; it just means that you were lax in your training.

If you are having trouble in this training routine check the following points:

1. Are you using the dog's name when you give him the "stay" command? Don't!

2. When you jerk the leash to correct him, are you pulling it straight up, which is correct, or toward you, which is wrong?

3. Are you praising him for staying put? Don't. Save your praise until this part of the lesson is over.

4. Do you give the hand signal to stay when you leave your dog?

5. Did you spend enough time teaching him the meaning of "stay," so the dog knows what you want of him?

6. Are you getting excited and confusing the dog? If so, better call off the lesson for today, but first do some heeling so you'll have a chance to praise the dog for his efforts.

Come To Heel

At the conclusion of every exercise in an obedience show, the judge says "Finish." The handler says "Heel," and the dog whips sharply over to the sitting position alongside his left leg. At least, that's the way it should happen.

What you're aiming for now is to have your dog come to the heel position every time he hears the command "Heel." With a well-trained animal, that command should work even when he gets all set to take off after a cat or to fight another dog.

There are several methods of teaching the dog to come to heel that are used by dog trainers. Here we'll explain what we think is the simplest way, and one that should work with most dogs.

Sit the dog facing you. Hold the leash loosely. Give the command "heel" and walk forward past the dog on his right side. As soon as the dog is alongside you, stop. Tell the dog to stay, step in front of him and repeat this three or four times. The first few times you may have to take a few steps before the dog is in heel position. When you think he's beginning to get the idea, stand in front of him, say "heel" and jerk him sharply around to your side. Pull up on the leash to make him sit. Each time you do this, say the "heel" loudly—in your command tone of voice. You may find this easier if you move your left foot backwards and then bring it forward as you wheel the dog into heel position.

No dog is too small to be trained. This little fellow is sitting on command, waiting for the next order from his trainer.

If you want to teach your dog to lie down from the sitting position, use a combination of verbal command with the hand technique illustrated here. Force him down gently to show him what you want, while at the same time repeating the word "Down."

This part of the dog's training will probably work up a good sweat on you, because you'll be doing all the work until he gets the idea down pat. Praise him as he begins to come to heel by himself.

If You Have A Big Dog

If your dog is one of the larger breeds you may find it easier to teach him the other way of coming to heel. He should walk around you from the right side and come to heel at your left. This will call for a lot of leash-juggling on your part, because you"ll have to shift the leash from your right hand to your left as the dog passes behind you. Otherwise you'll find yourself wrapped up in the leash.

Whichever method of coming to heel you use, be certain to *jerk* the leash when you correct the dog. Don't pull it. A dog that's dragged into heel position rather than guided by sharp jerks of the leash will find it harder to learn what his master wants of him.

Don't get too optimistic now. You may become too anxious to show off your dog's ability to get into heel position and work him off-lead before he's ready for that freedom. Have your dog letter-perfect in coming to heel with the leash before you work him free. If you want to do a little fancy training at this point, try teaching your dog to come to heel position from in front of you by using a slight motion of your left hand as the signal, instead of the voice command.

First use the voice command and the hand signal together, guiding the dog with jerks on the leash. After a while, he'll make the connection and you'll get him to heel by the hand signal alone.

"Down, Dog!"

Despite the fact that a dog seems to spend most of his life lying down, getting him to lie down on command and to stay down is one of the more difficult parts of dog training.

This calls for a battle of wills, often physical stress between the dog and his trainer, and a knowledge of dog psychology. Your dog's individual response will determine whether you use a frontal or a side attack to get him down.

The first problem is get your dog down. First try it from the front. Sit your dog facing you. Try pulling his front legs forward as you push down on his back to force him to the floor or the ground. Do this a few times, each time giving the command "Down" without using the dog's name. After some struggling, he may associate the command with his position. If he puts up too much of a struggle, try kneeling alongside him, on the left side, and dumping him on the ground by pulling his feet out to the right. Keep him down by placing a hand on his shoulder and repeat the command "Down."

If you find that neither of these approaches gets you anywhere, try using the leash. Slip the chain collar around so that the loose part hangs straight down. Sit the dog in front of you, and put your right foot over the leash so that you can slide it up under your instep. Say "Down" and pull firmly on the leash. That will bring the dog's head down. Then push his rear end down with your left hand and hold him down. He'll probably raise a fuss, but you just have to be firm and show him that he can't win. As soon as he lies quietly give the command "Stay" and try to keep him down.

Once you have brought your dog to the point where he goes down, you can use the leash to speed up his response. Hold the leash in your left hand with a little slack in it. When you give the command "Down," bring your right foot down on the leash to force the dog's head down and hold it down.

You should also begin to train your dog to drop on the hand signal.

Get your dog all the way down. Keep repeating "Down" while using the leash to pull him down. If he resists, pull harder on the leash. Even a large dog can be made to obey.

Extend your right arm in front of you whenever you give the verbal command "Down." You'll be surprised how soon your dog will learn to connect the hand signal with the "down" command. He should learn to drop down on either the hand or voice signal. Remember, the foot on leash, hand and voice all working together will show results on any dog, but you have to put in time and repetition on this exercise.

To make this more interesting for the dog, and easier on yourself, alternate sitting and lying down practice, and mix in some "down and stays" with your "sit and stay" drill. The "stay" signal for the downed dog is the same as for the sitting dog, a sweeping motion of the left hand, palm towards the dog's nose, and the verbal command "Stay."

Above all, don't let the dog get the idea that he doesn't have to go down unless he wants to. This is one other argument that you must win to have a trained dog. On the other hand, some dogs seem to find getting down a lot of fun. Then they proceed to roll over on their backs and wave their paws in the air. If yours tries that, jerk him up, get him down again and show him that this isn't a game, but serious training.

Some dogs become "creepers" who inch their way along the ground. If your dog inches toward you, move forward and reprimand him. If he moves away from you, he may be showing a sign of fear and it's a clue to ease up a

After a while, your dog should drop to the "down" position as soon as he hears the verbal command to drop. You can see that this dog is all keyed up, with his muscles tense, but he's staying down.

little on his training or to give him a word of encouragement and shift to another exercise.

When your dog is fairly good at lying down on command or signal, try him off leash. Put him in sitting position, step back about six feet and give him the "down" command. When he's reached that stage, work on the "down and stay." "Down" your dog, tell him to stay and step over him, then walk away. Finally "down and stay" him and step out of sight. When you do this, however, do not disappear behind him. Walk away in a direction in which he can see you go, so that he'll be able to watch the place for your eventual re-appearance.

Teach him to go down in heel position as well as facing you. A good practice is to walk your dog at heel position, stop, and command him to drop. Then give him the stay signal and leave him. While he's down, walk back and forth, step over him, bounce balls around and create other distractions, just as you did in teaching the sit-stay.

In teaching the dog to go down and to stay down, be careful of two points:

1. Do not use the dog's name in giving the command; use the word "down" or the hand signal. Use the word "stay" and hand signal to keep him down.

2. Do not praise him while he is down or he'll take that to mean that it's okay to jump up. When you want him to get up, say "Good dog," or some other words of approval, then pet and praise him. Don't expect him to go from a "down" position to heel at first. That's a pretty complicated maneuver for a dog that's just learning his obedience routines.

Stand On Command

When you're walking your dog in the rain, you may not want him to sit every time you stop. The solution is to teach him to stand on command. You can do that without confusing him, so that he'll sit without any command when you halt and will remain standing when you give the command.

To teach this, walk the dog in the regular heeling manner, but hold the leash rather short in your right hand. When you stop, say "Stand." At the same time, pull the leash tight, but do not jerk it—the jerk is the command to sit. Before the dog begins to sit, slide your left hand down under him, or use your foot on a very small dog, and praise him. If he starts to sit, move a step forward, repeat "Stand" and praise him. It may be necessary to loop the end of the leash around the dog's body and hold him up until he gets the idea that "stand" means that he must not sit.

Alternate the stand practice with regular heel sits so that the dog will get the idea of the difference between the commands and what's expected of him for each. If he starts to move while standing, correct him with a firm "No" and repeat "Stand." If he starts moving before you have a chance to stop him, take a few steps with him and then give the "stand" command again.

By now, your dog should know the "stay" hand signal, so try giving him the order to stay while he is standing. Then walk to the end of the leash. Keep him standing, circle him back to heel position and praise him. Then try dropping the leash and doing the same thing; finally stand him off-lead and walk around him, away from him, and back to heel position.

One of the required show routines is "Stand for Examination," in which the handler "stands" the dog and walks away from him. Then the judge walks over and runs his hand over the dog's head and back. During this, the dog must not show any resentment — judges dislike being bitten — and must not even move his feet until the handler is told by the judge to return to his dog. In time, your dog should be able to stand for from three to five minutes without moving.

Some trainers of small dogs have found it easier to teach them to stand if they are placed on a table until they get the idea, and then practice standing on ground level.

It's good training for the dog if you can get someone he doesn't know to "examine" him while he is standing. At first let a stranger merely touch his head and back. As he gets more used to being handled the stranger can run his hands over the dog's entire body.

When standing on command is being practiced, always get yourself into the habit of returning to the dog by circling him from the right and returning to heel position.

There are a number of tactics you can use if your dog won't remain standing. You can put a long leash on him and have someone standing a distance behind him pull back if he starts to move, while you correct him. Some trainers forget to step forward with the *right* foot when they leave the dog. Many dogs associate a motion of the left foot with the signal to start walking.

If the signal to stay is not respected by your dog, you can make it a bit more drastic by slapping him firmly on the snout when you give him the signal to stay on his four feet. You might also try standing your dog and then leaving the room, with someone watching to reprimand him if he moves or tries to follow you.

Come On Command

Pages ago, we spoke of the "coaxing" voice. When you begin teaching your dog to come to you when you call him, put all the coaxing you can into your voice. Sit your dog, tell him to "stay" and step to the end of the leash. Use your dog's name and the command "Come." Stretch out the word "come," and say it with affection. At the same time, give the leash a sharp tug to start your dog toward you. He may want to come to heel position, but sit him down facing you, and try to get him to sit straight directly in front of you. To correct his sit, don't try to juggle him around, but take a step backward and put him in the proper position. Most important now, however, is to get him to *come*. Make a big fuss over him and praise him, even if it means that he'll jump up from his sitting position—you can correct that later. Then call him to heel position, and praise him again.

As soon as he comes and sits in front of you when you call him, try it off-lead from a short distance. Then make the distances longer, until you are calling him from 40 or 50 feet—and he comes. However, if he runs away, even once, or gambols around instead of coming directly to you, put him back on leash and work with him until he gets to the point of coming and sitting down in front of you whenever you call "Come." Don't stand for any nonsense. Make him understand that "come" means exactly that, and immediately. Sometimes it may be helpful to tie a 20-foot cord to his collar and use that as a leash to pull him to you when you call him.

Don't try this exercise outdoors until he is 100 per cent perfect in response indoors, on and off leash. A bad habit formed at this stage of training

When you first train your dog to come, use your best coaxing voice and try to make him want to come to you. When he does, lavish affection on him and reward him with praise.

can be hard to cure later, so don't be in too much of a hurry to begin working him off-lead.

Heeling Free

As soon as your friends begin to compliment you on how well your dog works with the leash, you can start working him without it, letting him heel free alongside you. Before you give him full freedom, however, let him become accustomed to less leash control. Instead of holding the leash, throw it over your right shoulder. When necessary, use your left hand to jerk the leash and correct your dog.

When you first let your dog work free, keep his attention by constantly talking to him. If he lags, call him up to you. If he begins to go ahead, don't run after him but come to a stop and call him to heel. Since he may become bored with training, use your imagination to keep him interested. Don't just

This is a big step forward — working the dog off leash. Always carry the leash with you in case you should need it. Remember to keep talking to your dog to keep his attention focused on you.

walk with him alongside you. Vary your pace. Speed up, slow down to a very slow walk, stop frequently and have him sit.

Don't walk him for more than five minutes at a time. Try the other exercises he has learned. Occasionally put the leash back on to give him some guidance. When the leash is off, the dog should be controlled by voice commands, and be careful to use the same words and the tone of voice to which he has become accustomed. A series of new commands such as "Get back here," "Slow down!," "Where do you think you're going?" will throw him into utter confusion.

Whenever the situation gets too messed up, just stop, call the dog back to heel and start off again. If he gets excited and begins running around, sometimes the voice command "down" will work. Then walk over to him, attach the leash and review his heeling-on-leash routine.

Sometimes you can fool your dog. Get a piece of fishing line, attach it to his collar and walk him through his exercises. He'll forget that he's tied to you and the corrections that come to him unexpectedly may be very effective.

No matter how well trained you think your dog is, never walk him without carrying the leash in case you may need it.

You can make the heel-free practice fun for yourself and your dog. When you are walking together, play with him. As you get to know your dog better through training him, you'll discover the things he likes. Some breeds, such as Boxers, like to have their flews (the overhang of the lip) twitched as they walk; others may enjoy a quick scratch behind the ears.

Carrying a pocketful of dog candy or dog biscuits may hold your dog's attention better than anything else. Some dogs take their training very seriously and prefer not to be bothered when they're concentrating on heeling or other routines. Very often a lagging dog can be speeded up if you make a show of enthusiasm. Put excitement in your voice when you give commands; jump up and down in excitement when you call him.

Losing your temper if your dog runs away during his first heel-free session won't help the situation. If he ignores your commands to come, and if "down" doesn't work, try arousing his curiosity. Take something out of your pocket, begin playing with it and walk away. Chances are he'll come bounding over to see what's doing. When he comes close to you, don't grab for him or use your leash as a whip. Sooner or later you'll have your hands on him, and when you do, give him a good, long lesson, making your corrections with the leash as strong as your physical strength (and your conscience) allows.

If his running away consists of running into the street or highway, then training rules are suspended and he deserves whatever he gets. A spanked dog is far better off than one that has been hit by a truck.

As soon as your dog works well indoors, promote him to outdoor exercises, but let him understand that training is serious business.

5. Advanced Obedience Training

Whether or not you plan to try to earn an obedience certificate by entering your dog in a show, it's a good idea to try him on advanced obedience training just to see how well the two of you can work together. Here's what advanced obedience training covers:

1. Heel free
2. Drop on recall
3. Retrieve dumbbell from the ground (or floor)
4. Retrieve dumbbell over a hurdle
5. Broad jump
6. Long sit (three minutes with handler out of sight)
7. Long down (five minutes with handler out of sight)

Heel free we've discussed, and the more you practice it, the better you and your dog will work together.

Drop On Recall

Drop on recall is a combination of two exercises you've already been working on: the Come or Recall, and the Down. In this routine, you leave the dog in a sitting position and walk across the room or the judging ring. Call the dog with voice or signal, and when he is about halfway to you, or at the judge's signal, command him to drop. Then you call him again. He should come to you, sit in front of you, wait for your signal, and then go to heel position on your command.

Training in that routine, as in any other, should begin with the leash. Sit your dog and walk away to the end of the leash, facing him, holding the leash in your left hand. Say "Come" and run backwards—first making sure the way is clear. Now you need some agility. While still moving backwards and with the dog a leash-length away, give the "down" command. If your dog doesn't drop, try to catch the leash with your right foot and force him down. When he drops, give the order to stay and back away. Wait a minute or so and then repeat the procedure.

When he drops fairly regularly on command, try this routine without the leash. Sit your dog, leave him (remembering to give him the "stay" command

Practice the sit-stay. Sit your dog. Give him the "stay" signal, back away slowly and keep him in the sitting position.

and to start off on your right foot). Face him from a distance and call him. Then shout "Down" or give him the upraised hand signal to drop. If you don't get a quick response, then run toward him and make him get down. Some dogs will run off to one side when they are given the command to drop. If that happens, it just means more work with the leash to steady your dog.

You'll probably find that your dog will soon slow down to a walk on his recalls, waiting for his command to drop. To remedy that, don't command him to drop every time, and do not always drop him in the same place or the same distance from you. When you call him, put a lot of coaxing in your voice. You may even have to jump up and down when you call him to excite

57

him to a fast recall, or have a piece of candy or morsel of food as a reward when he comes quickly. If you find that your dog stops on the way in whether you command him to drop or not, then skip the drop for a while and just practice straight recalls.

Dumbbell Retrieving

What's hard about teaching a dog to pick up a dumbbell and bring it back to you? You'll find out when you start working your dog on this exercise. A dog that enjoys running after sticks and balls will sometimes develop a positive dislike for doing the same thing with a dumbbell just because you want him to.

This part of training seems much easier to the beginning trainer than it really is. Sometimes it takes an experienced dog handler six months or a year to get a dog to work reliably with his dumbbell. Don't make the mistake of thinking that you can short-cut this part of your dog's training by just throwing out a dumbbell and having him bring it to you.

First Step — "Hold It!"

The first step is to teach your dog to hold the dumbbell in his mouth. Sit your dog. Place the end of the leash on the ground so that it doesn't leave much play when you step on it. This gives you both hands free to work with dumbbell and the dog. Open your dog's mouth and put the dumbbell in, but do not force it in by pressing it against his teeth. Be sure that the dog's lips are pulled back so he will not bite them. Getting the dumbbell in is only part of the problem. Use the command "Take it!" when you give him the dumbbell and then press his jaws together against it so he can't drop it, and tell him to "Hold it." Most dogs, even the smallest, will put up a good fight against holding the dumbbell the first few times, so don't expect an easy victory. Praise the dog while the dumbbell is in his mouth, even if he's trying like mad to get rid of it. When you take the dumbbell out of his mouth say "Give it!" or "Out." Sometimes, just to be different, the dog will refuse to give up the dumbbell. If that happens, don't get involved in a tug-of-war. The idea is to force him to give up the object. Try to pry his jaws apart while commanding "Give," or "Out" in a firmer tone. Blowing in his nostrils may induce him to relinquish it, or a sharp slap on the side of the nose may bring results.

Try to win the argument. Your dog may scream with rage or pull away with all his strength to avoid having the dumbbell placed in his mouth. While you have your foot on the tight leash, you have control of the dog. If he tries to rear up on his hind legs, use the leash to pull him down. Make every effort to force him to keep the dumbbell long enough for you to praise him for it. Eventually you will win the dispute and the dog will hold the dumbbell. If he drops it immediately, put it back in his mouth. Sometimes you can force him to hold it by looping the leash under his jaw and the dumbbell and leading him around for a few minutes with a very tight leash. When your dog

One of the first steps in the Dumbbell Retrieve is to teach your dog to hold an object in his mouth on command. Will he hold it when the trainer removes her hand?

sits quietly in the sit-stay position with the dumbbell in his mouth while you walk around him, then you've won that round, but don't expect a one-round victory. And don't carry on the dumbbell vs. dog fight for more than five minutes or so. If you can't win, then shift to some other exercise that the dog likes and end the session on a friendlier note—if you can.

Now, "Take It!"

Next step, to get your dog to take the dumbbell willingly. While experts can use the choke collar to force the dog to take it, your best bet is to try to coax and tease him into going for the object. Heel your dog while you hold the dumbbell in your right hand. Wave it in front of him, encourage him to jump for it, and when he takes it, walk more rapidly, hoping that he'll hold it. Take it away from him while you are heeling and let him jump for it again. Try to make this a game of fun instead of a lesson. When you have him all excited, sit him and see whether he'll take the dumbbell willingly. In due time, he should. But be patient. You should plan on spending a month or two just getting your dog to take the dumbbell from your hand and hold it without dropping it. But don't neglect the other training during that time. Keep on practicing your heeling, on leash and free, and the drop on recall. On days when you are tired or grouchy, just skip the dumbbell routine and concentrate on the other work.

Sometimes the dumbbell is at fault. Your pet shop will usually have a dumbbell of the proper size for your breed of dog, but sometimes a dog will prefer a larger or smaller dumbbell than the one he should be using. If your dog seems to prefer to carry the dumbbell by the end block instead of by the bar, get another dumbbell with a longer bar or larger end blocks. Some dogs will try to chew the wooden bar of the dumbell, but you can cover that part with electrician's tape or leather to stop the chewing. It wasn't until the sixth dumbbell or so that this writer's dog decided she was satisfied with the object and began to pick it up by the bar and carry it.

Let's Carry It

Finally, your dog will hold the dumbbell. When he reaches that stage of training, try to convince him that he should carry it for you. Sit him facing you with the dumbbell in his mouth and walk back about a leash-length. Call your dog and keep saying "Hold it." If he drops the dumbbell make him take it immediately. Let him know that you are displeased when he drops it. Have him sit in front of you again with the dumbbell in his mouth. Then start off on a fast heel. The dog should heel with you, holding the dumbbell. Don't, however, expect him to carry it for more than a minute or two. Take it away. Let him have it again. Try to make a game of dumbbell-carrying. Keep on with this program until your dog can be made to sit and stay holding the dumbbell, then come on command carrying it, and finally sit in front of you, still holding it.

If you find that your dog carries the dumbbell loosely in his mouth,

A well poised dog is a well trained dog. This Doberman Pinscher is perfectly posed awaiting a signal from his master.

tap the ends with your fingers. The wobbling effect should make him take a tighter grip on it. If he thinks the dumbbell is a chewing toy, correct him by closing his jaws over it and holding them shut for a few seconds, meanwhile telling him "No!"

While you're engaged in this dumbbell training, try to fix the command "Take it!" in the dog's mind. Vary the game by using old gloves, sticks, large pieces of hard rubber and other objects of the right carrying-size that are around. Use the expression "Take it!" when you hand him a piece of candy or biscuit. That will give the sound a pleasant association in his mind. If your dog is large enough you can begin teaching him to carry small bags or packages back from the store when you go shopping. Be patient. This training takes a lot of time, but after some weeks your dog will take whatever you hand him and hold it, carry it, and give it up when you put your hand down and say "Give it" or "Out."

Retrieving On Command

The next stage: to get your dog to go out, pick up the dumbbell and bring it back to you. How long will this take? That depends both on you and the dog. A rare dog will get the idea in a few lessons, the average dog will take from one to two months, a stubborn dog may take several months, but almost any dog can be taught to do this if you stick to the project.

Your objective is to train your dog to the point where you can sit him at heel, say "Stay," throw out the dumbbell, say "Take it," and have him run out, pick it up and return to sit in front of you with the dumbbell in his mouth, waiting for you to take it from him.

Start this training while walking your dog. Hold the dumbbell close to the ground, just in front of him, and urge him to take it. If you get no response, try commanding him to "Take it!" at the same time jerking the leash forward hard. By trial and error you can probably find a way to get your dog more interested in the dumbbell. Make believe you are going to throw it, or pretend to hide it behind your back. Sometimes placing it in front of the dog and kicking it a few feet away will get him to jump for it. You can have someone pull the dumbbell away from the dog with a piece of string or fishline, while you are encouraging him to go after it. If nothing seems to work, go back to putting the dumbbell into the dog's mouth yourself, but praise him as if he had done it. During this part of his training, let everything else drop from the agenda. Don't try to make him heel properly or come to sit with the dumbbell when he does pick it up. Just work at trying to get him to pick up that (censored) object.

And most important, do all this work on leash. The dog may occasionally pick up the dumbbell if you let it fly off and he's running free, but that doesn't mean that he's learning. He's just playing. Until he takes it while on leash, he has not been trained.

You will find that your dog will probably have relapses during this phase of his training. For a day or two he'll pick up the dumbbell every time, then he'll backslide and ignore it completely. Keep on trying. Eventually you'll reach the point where he'll go out for the dumbbell and pick it up 90 per cent of the time. Even dogs that have been trained for years will sometimes get an idea in their heads and refuse to touch the thing—usually when they're in a show with a hundred spectators watching the performance.

Many persons give up dog training at this stage—and you can't really blame them, because for weeks and weeks they seem to be making no progress whatever. If you feel that it just isn't worth the effort, skip the following pages and turn to the final chapter, "Training for Fun." Perhaps you'll pick up the dumbbell some day and try again.

But if you're still with us, let's continue the Retrieve on Command. With your dog on leash, throw the dumbbell about eight or ten feet in front of you. With excited shouts of "Take it," run out with your dog to the dumbbell and hope that he pounces on it. If he does, run backwards, make the dog

Good boy! Bringing back the dummy shows that this dog is getting the idea of retrieving — especially important for hunting dogs like this Labrador.

Dogs can be trained to do just about anything . . . if you have the time and patience to teach them properly.

sit in front of you with the dumbbell in his mouth, take it from him, and send him to heel position. When the dog picks up the dumbbell most of the time when he's on leash, try the same thing off leash. During this off-leash work, use your voice commands to keep the dog under control.

Throw the dumbbell farther away and in different directions. Try placing it on the ground ten feet or so away and sending your dog after it. Don't work the dog too long on this at any one session. If he picks it up two or three times, switch over to some other exercise.

Alternate work on leash and off leash. The dog that has been trained to pick up the dumbbell and bring it when he is leashed will invariably work better when he is running free.

Now, let's look at some of the common problems that may show up during dumbbell retrieving.

The slow-poke: Some dogs will amble out at the rate of about two miles a day and perform the routine in slow motion. This may often be corrected if you get more excitement into your commands. As soon as your dog picks up the dumbbell, jump up and down and clap your hands to bring him back faster. Put him back on leash, run out with him and drag him back at a rapid pace, with words of encouragement. Wave the dumbbell in front of his nose before you throw it to get him keyed up.

The anticipator: Some dogs won't wait for the command to "Take it!" but will run out as soon as the dumbbell is thrown. Put your foot on the leash and throw the dumbbell out while telling the dog to stay. Use the hand signal and slap him on the nose if he tries to move before you give the command.

The dumbbell spitter: Many dogs will go out, pick up the dumbbell, return with it, and spit it out as soon as they return to their trainer. Use voice corrections for this. Shout "Hold it!" as soon as the dog approaches you with the dumbbell in his mouth. If necessary, use your hands to keep the dumbbell in his mouth until you take it.

The disinterested: Sometimes the dog just watches you throw the dumbbell and won't even go out after it. A slight boot in the rear end may get him started. However, with a more sensitive or nervous dog, that means a return to more work on leash to get the idea across. Other dogs will run out to the dumbbell and just stand over it without trying to take it. If your dog does that, run out, put the dumbbell in his mouth and run backwards to the starting position calling him after you.

The playboy: A few dogs will run out, pick up the dumbbell and then proceed to dash off in any direction. The best correction for that should come from some person other than the trainer. Have another person shout at the dog when he does that and make him run back to you; meanwhile you call him in the old, coaxing voice.

Jumping On Command

Training your dog to jump on command is fun and it is one of the easiest parts of his advanced obedience training. Your dog should be able

This little fellow isn't getting anywhere. To get him over, his trainer better do some jumping himself. Once the first jump has been made, the rest is easier.

to clear a hurdle that is one and one-half times his shoulder height, unless you have a Great Dane, St. Bernard or other huge dog. They should be able to clear a jump that's three feet high, or at least their own height at the shoulder. If you want, you can build or buy a solid hurdle jump, or you can use a carpenter's wooden saw horse or make your own hurdle of plywood or beaverboard, or even heavy cardboard. A convenient hedge of the right height makes a good hurdle for jumping.

When you first start jump training, begin on a fairly low hurdle—low, that is, for the size of your dog. Lead him to the hurdle, give him a good chance to examine it, then lead him about ten feet away and run over to it with him. As you reach the hurdle, command "Over" or "Hup!" and jerk the leash upward. If your dog balks, then lead him back to the hurdle and go over it yourself, calling him to follow you. Every time you jump your dog use the same command, in a coaxing voice at first, then in the "command" tone of voice. As soon as your dog gets into the spirit of jumping, try sitting him about fifteen feet from the hurdle and give him the jump command.

Then call him back over the hurdle to come and sit in front of you. You may need the help of another person at this time to make sure he comes back over the hurdle and not around it. You'll find that your dog will need a much shorter run than you'd think to clear the hurdle. Most breeds seem to stop just short of the hurdle, bunch their muscles and soar over.

To add zest to the jumping practice — and to prepare for the next training step—put the dumbbell in the dog's mouth when you send him over the jump and make him hold it until he comes back and sits in front of you.

Retrieve Over Obstacle

Sorry, you're in for more dumbbell problems. This exercise calls for the dog to leave you on command, jump over the hurdle, pick up a dumbbell you have thrown over it, jump back over the hurdle with the dumbbell in his mouth and come to a sit in front of you—still carrying the dumbbell.

Again, back to the leash. Stand about five feet in front of the hurdle and tell the dog to stay. Throw the dumbbell over the hurdle after waving it around to make sure that the dog's attention is focused on it. Then in rapid sequence order him to "Hup" or "Over," "Take it!" Then, making a rapid about-turn, lead the dog back over the hurdle to sit in front of you. Take the dumbbell, praise the dog, and repeat several times. Most dogs seem to enjoy

He's over with the dumbbell, but before that a lot of work went into training this little Dachshund. Now all he has to do is bring it back to his trainer, wait for it to be taken, and go to heel position when commanded.

this exercise and will soon go through the routine after the one command of "Take it." When your dog gets that down pat, make him stay at your side for a few seconds before you send him over the hurdle. Vary your manner of throwing the dumbbell. Send it a distance away from the hurdle, throw it as close to the hurdle as you can, throw it off to either side of the hurdle. If your dog acts up on this exercise, then back to the leash again for more corrections.

One problem encountered in this exercise by some trainers is that the dog will jump the hurdle, run over to the dumbbell and just stand there. For that too, try to get another person to help you by "shouting" your dog back to you over the hurdle, with the dumbbell in his mouth. If you call him back, he may get the idea that he's supposed to wait for another command before bringing it back. If you don't have assistance, run out to the dog, encourage him to pick up the dumbbell, run back with him, making sure he jumps the hurdle, and then push him down to a sit in front of you.

Don't be too particular at first about the way he sits. Just work on having him jump the hurdle, get the dumbbell and return with it. Refinements can be developed later.

The Broad Jump

Using the same command, "Hup" or "Over," you can train your dog to do the broad jump. In an obedience show, the dog is required to jump a distance that is twice the height of his hurdle jump. The broad jump hurdles are 6 feet long, and 5½ inches tall at the lowest or front end, 8½ inches tall at the far end. With those figures in mind you can probably make a good substitute over which to jump your dog.

In this exercise the dog sits at your side in heel position. You leave him and walk to the side of the hurdle. Then you give him the command. He must clear the broad jump. As he is in the air, you turn so that you are facing him. He must come to a sit in front of you and wait for your command to come to heel position.

You'll get some exercise, too, in preparing your dog for the broad jump. Keep him on leash and sit him about six feet in front of a fairly short broad jump. Giving the command "Hup" or "Over," start for the jump at a good fast pace and jump over it with your dog. As soon as you land, shout "Come" and pull him to a sit in front of you. Repeat, repeat and repeat, timing your voice with the action. When you think your dog is ready, sit him off leash and go through the maneuver with him again a few times. Make sure that he jumps straight over the hurdle, not cutting the corner of the jump. Then, let the dog take the jump a few times alone. Leave him just as you reach the hurdle; call him to you as soon as he lands. Finally, sit the dog, leave him, stand by the hurdle, give him the command to jump. He should come to the sitting position in front of you with no further command. If he pulls any boners, more leash work.

For some fun-practice, set up the broad jump and high jump and heel the dog at a fast pace off leash. Have him jump the hurdles and return to your side as you trot around in a big circle. Remember that the dog needs a longer take-off run for the broad jump than he does for the high jump.

Normally a dog enjoys jumping so he has no serious problems in picking up the idea of the broad jump. He may, however, figure out that it's easier to walk through the hurdles than to jump them, or he may circle around them. That means more work on leash with some good, healthy jerks to get him started on the jump.

If your dog won't come to a sit in front of you after he jumps, try your coaxing voice to get him there. If he anticipates the command and jumps too soon, confuse him a little. Leave him a few times, walk over to the hurdle and watch him. If you see him getting ready to take off, order him to stay. Then walk back to heel position without making him jump.

If he has a habit of running wide after he lands instead of coming directly to you, then make him practice more jumps on leash and pull him in sharply each time. For variety, you can teach your dog to jump over a stick that you hold in your hand. You'll find the broad jump training handy on a rainy day when you can order your pet to jump over a puddle instead of dragging you around it, or through it.

The Long Sit And Down

In advanced obedience work — what the dog shows call the Open Class — the final exercise consists of a three-minute sit with the handler out of sight and a five-minute down with the handler out of sight.

This dog has been commanded to sit and stay. Even the offer of a bone won't get him up until the trainer says "Take it."

69

For that, just practice giving your dog the command to sit or lie down and to stay and leave him. Provide the distractions discussed earlier, and be sure to give lots of praise to the dog for staying down alone. However, make it a practice to return to the heel position while he is still sitting or lying down. Then after a few seconds tell him "okay," and when he jumps up praise or reward him.

Where Do You Go From Here?

Under usual conditions, working with a cooperative dog and starting his training at about eight months of age, it should take about another eight months to reach the stage where you can expect him to have acquired the obedience training described. You can be justly proud of your dog if he can go through these obedience routines. They show that you have helped your dog develop his natural abilities and you now have a useful dog who has his own interests in life.

If you are interested in having your dog earn obedience awards or degrees, you can enter him in Obedience Trials sanctioned by the American Kennel Club. These trials are open to any purebred dog that is registered with the A.K.C. In many cities, the American Society for the Prevention of Cruelty to Animals conducts training classes and holds more "democratic" shows in which any dog may be entered, even if he's of mixed ancestry and not an A.K.C. blueblood. For information, contact your local A.S.P.C.A. For information on the Kennel Club obedience trials, with a complete description of the tests and how they are conducted, write to Foley Dog Shows, Inc., 2009 Ranstead Street, Philadelphia, Pennsylvania, and ask for a free copy of "Regulations and Standards for Obedience Trials." In back of this booklet, you'll find plans for making the "official" hurdles for high and broad jumps.

The training for the highest obedience classes, Utility and Tracking, is not covered in this book. It is almost impossible for a beginning dog trainer — or even for one with limited experience — to prepare a dog for that type of work without attending dog-training classes or turning his dog over to a professional trainer. For information on the dog-training classes in your area, again turn to the A.S.P.C.A., or write to the Gaines Dog Research Center, 250 Park Avenue, New York, New York, for a list of the dog-training schools in the United States.

Obedience Trials

The purpose of dog obedience trials is to demonstrate the usefulness of dogs as companions and guardians. Most of the large dog shows include obedience classes and many clubs in different parts of the country conduct yearly obedience trials.

The A.K.C. trials are divided into four general classes: Novice, Open, Utility and Tracking.

The Novice and Open classes are divided into Class A for owner-handlers

They've been told to sit and stay, and they're staying. If possible, train a group of dogs at the same time so they'll learn to obey when other dogs are around. That's one advantage of attending obedience classes.

and Class B for amateur and professional handlers. Utility and Tracking classes are not divided.

To see how good your dog is at obedience work you would first enter him in the Novice class, where he will be judged on the following basis:

Test	Maximum Points
1. Heel on leash	35
2. Stand for examination by judge	30
3. Heel free — off leash	45
4. Recall	30
5. One-minute sit	30
6. Three-minute down	30
Maximum possible score	200

After "qualifying" in three different shows in which he earns at least 170 points, and 50 per cent or more of the points for each test, your dog receives a certificate from the American Kennel Club awarding him the "Companion Dog" degree and the right to use the letters "C.D." after his name.

71

After he earns his "C.D." you can both go on to further honors — the "C.D.X." — Companion Dog Excellent — degree. For that your dog must qualify in three trials in the Open Class, on these tests:

Test	Maximum Points
1. Heel free	40
2. Drop on recall	30
3. Retrieve on flat	25
4. Retrieve over obstacle	35
5. Broad jump	20
6. Three-minute sit	25
7. Five-minute down	25
Maximum Possible Score	200

After winning his "C.D.X." your dog may be entered in the Utility Class where his performance will be judged on these tests (which are described in full in the Foley Dog Shows booklet):

Test	Maximum Points
1. Scent discrimination — article no. 1	20
2. Scent discrimination — article no. 2	20
3. Scent discrimination — article no. 3	20
4. Seek back	30
5. Signal exercise	35
6. Directed jumping	40
7. Group examination	35
Maximum Possible Score	200

A dog that qualifies for this title receives the proud honor of being known as "Utility Dog" and can carry the initials "U.D." after his name.

For the final obedience degree, "Tracking," the dog must follow the trail of a stranger for at least 440 yards and find an object he had dropped. First the dog must be certified as ready for the tracking test by a judge, then he must complete a tracking test in which there are two judges and three or more dogs compete.

You can be sure that the dog carrying U.D.T. after his or her name is quite an animal!

6. Training for Fun

As a relief from the rigid obedience training — or just for fun — teach your dog a few tricks for his amusement and yours. It's surprising, but the dog will recognize the difference between "fun" tricks and obedience training — possibly reflecting the difference in your attitude. In teaching tricks be more generous with dog candy or other tidbits.

Almost every dog can be taught to beg, shake hands, roll over, jump through a hoop, play dead, or ask for his dinner. However, don't rush a young puppy into trying to learn tricks before he is old enough to get the idea and physically able to perform the tricks you demand of him.

Begging

"Begging" comes naturally to many breeds, particularly Dachshunds. Some dogs have a poorer sense of balance than others and begging may come harder to them. A young puppy often does not have the muscular development to be able to sit and beg. Strangely, long-bodied dogs have no greater difficulty in sitting up on their hindquarters than do other breeds.

How you train your dog to beg depends on his disposition. Some dogs will allow you to hold their front feet and help them to a sitting position. Others will back away if you touch their feet. If your dog is a "don't hold my feet" type, take him by the collar from a sitting position and raise him gently. Hold him in position for a few seconds, give him a reward and some praise and then let him down. If the dog associates begging with pleasant eating, he'll learn it much faster. When you are teaching him to beg use some word or expression to tie in with the act, like "Beg," "Ask," "Say please" or "Up." If you are training your dog in obedience be careful not to use a word that you also use as an obedience command.

As soon as he begins to get the idea, try him by holding a piece of meat or other morsel just above his head. If he jumps for it, or tries to stand on his hind legs, say "No" and push him down.

As a variation on begging, you may be able to teach your dog to stand on his hind legs, balancing himself for a reward.

To teach your dog tricks is simple. Training must be repetitious and broken down into its simple elements, utilizing the same hand and voice commands over and over again until the dog associates the sounds with the meanings. Never speak harshly to your dog, but be firm. To teach your dog to beg, you must first teach him to sit properly.

Shake Hands

The most common dog trick is shaking hands, and it can be taught easily. Take the dog's collar in one hand, and with the other tap the underside of one of the dog's front paws. Command him to "Shake hands" or "Give a paw." Just as you give the command, pull the dog's collar sideways. That will pull him off balance and he will raise the loose paw into the air to get his balance. Take hold of that paw, shake it gently, praise the dog and reward him immediately. After doing that a few times the dog will get the idea.

Most dogs learn to raise a paw the moment a hand is lowered towards the floor or when they hear the command that means "shake." However, some become bored with this after a while and look for the reward before offering a paw. No reward in sight or scent and no paw is raised.

You can dress this trick up a bit by teaching your dog to give the other paw for a second shake. You can teach him to respond to a voice or hand signal that means "the other paw" after the first paw-shake. Be careful not

(Above) Then hold him in the position of "begging" until he gets the idea of what you want him to do. Finally he can beg by himself.

(Below) Any dog can learn to fetch—but the idea is to train your dog to retrieve the object quickly and upon command without damaging it.

Though you don't have to feed your dog at the table, this is a very nice trick if you can do it.

to overdo this trick. A dog will get as tired as a politician if he's expected to shake hands all day long with people he hardly knows.

Roll Over

First teach your dog to lie down on command. Then you can teach him to roll over. Attach his leash and sit him facing you. Give him the command to lie down. Then say "Roll Over" and make a circular motion with your right hand. Take the dog's underneath paw and flip him over to the right (on his left side). Hold him down for a moment, praise and reassure him, and repeat the lesson a few times. Combine the circular hand motion with the quick flip-over. The first few times the dog will be surprised at your antics and he will probably try to get up fast, but when he realizes that it's a game, he'll join in the fun. As soon as he begins to roll over by himself, you can start doing this trick without the leash. At first, keep the two motions, the "down" signal and the "roll over" signal, separate. After a while, the signal alone or the words alone will do the trick. However, don't tell him to roll over unless he is already down. Telling a standing dog to lie down and roll over is a bit too much for one message to accomplish.

Through The Hoop

In theory, any dog who has been trained to jump over a hurdle can be trained to jump through a hoop. Some suspicious-natured dogs will simply refuse to go through the hoop and the effort forcing them to do it just isn't worth while. Let's hope that your dog isn't prejudiced in advance against hoop-jumping.

For the first session, keep him on leash. Tell him to sit and stay. If he's curious about the hoop in your hand and wants to sniff at it and examine it, let him. Walk to the end of the leash, holding the hoop in your left hand, the

You can easily train your dog to jump through the hoop by first starting with the hoop very low and then increasing its height. How high you hold it depends on the size of your dog.

Training your dog to walk a narrow board is a lot of fun for both the dog and you. Some dogs take to this kind of training very readily — with others it is almost impossible to get them to walk and balance themselves.

leash in your right. Give the command to jump — "Hup" or "Over" — and jerk the leash to bring the dog forward and through the hoop. If he balks, put the edge of the hoop on the ground and let him walk through it. Once he has been through it, he's less likely to balk at jumping. It may be necessary, if the hoop is big enough, for *you* to crawl through it and pull the dog through after you.

Reward the dog each time he jumps through. When he has become adept enough at hoop-jumping to perform off-leash, you can hold a hoop in each hand and have the dog run circles around you, jumping through the hoops on each round, or you can hold two hoops a foot or so apart and have him jump through both at the same time. Another variation is to form a hoop with your arms and have your dog jump through — but that's not recommended for larger dogs.

Playing Dead

Playing dead is a further development of the "down" command. When the dog responds quickly to the upraised hand signal to drop, you can teach him to play dead. When he drops, turn him on his side and hold his muzzle flat on the floor while you repeat "Play dead" or "Dead dog" a number of times. Soon, the dog will stay down in that relaxed position. When he does, clap your hands or give him an "Okay, get up" command and reward him.

Speaking On Command

Some years ago, speaking on command was part of the obedience routine, but it has been dropped as a requirement. It's still fun to teach your dog to bark when you tell him to, and this trick has useful applications. Trying to find your dog in the dark will be much easier if he lets out a bark when he hears the command to "speak."

Teaching this to your dog is a matter of applied psychology and hardly two dogs, even from the same litter, can be taught in the same way. You can probably teach your dog by tempting him with a morsel of food, withdrawing it and saying "Speak" until he lets out a bark. Then praise him and repeat the lesson. But it's possible that all this will do is to start the dog drooling and snapping at the food.

Another way is to take advantage of the time when your dog does bark and get him to associate barking with the "speak" command. Many dogs will bark when tied. If that works with yours, try it. Fasten his leash to something and walk away. When he barks, praise him and reward him and be sure to get in your "speak" word of command.

Your dog is full of talent if you will only take the time and trouble to find out what he can do.

A dog that has been taught never to bark will be a problem. If yours is an apartment house dog, taught from puppyhood that barking is an offense, he may never learn to bark on command.

The basic idea, however, is to get him so keyed up that he will bark and to get him to connect barking with the sound of "speak" and with a reward. Try different approaches until you find the one that works for you.